FALLING OUT OF STEP

poems by

Carol Stevens Kner

Finishing Line Press
Georgetown, Kentucky

FALLING OUT OF STEP

Publisher: Leah Huete de Maines
Editor: Christen Kincaid
Cover Art: sparkia, iStock/Getty Images Plus via Getty Images
Author Photo: Mary Queen of Headshots Photography
              www.maryqueenofheadshots.com
Cover Design: Michele Trombley

Order online: www.finishinglinepress.com
              also available on amazon.com

Author inquiries and mail orders:
Finishing Line Press
P. O. Box 1626
Georgetown, Kentucky 40324
U. S. A.

Table of Contents

For Andrew, Annie, and Peter
who live in all the rooms of my heart.

I

For we have seen on our way and fallen in love
with the world that will pass in a twinkling.
—Czeslow Milosz, *Incantation*

Of Body and Mind

My love, so far we've managed to escape
life's bleak conspiracies: shipwreck and fire,
money squandered on some desperate hope,
the careless dispatch of a child to war.
But now just as our moon begins to rise,
old currents ruffle up a pirate breeze
that plunders some deep-buried treasure-trove
and fouls your rigging, sets your sails to luff.

For so subversive and malign a scheme,
contrariness will sing louder than blame.
Like maples on the brink of winter's storm,
let's flame red, meddling naysayers disarm,
refuse a passage straitened by regret
for one that's generous and full of light.

Erato Entertains

*Poets don't drive cars. Poets don't go to the supermarket. Poets don't
empty the garbage. Poets aren't on the P.T.A. Poets, you know, they
don't go picket the Better Housing Bureau of whatever. . . Poets don't
even speak on the telephone. Poets don't talk to anybody.*
    —Bob Dylan, *The New York Times*, January 9, 2000

I long to settle on the porch divan
my bare feet warming in a patch of sun
a French press brewing my second cup,
fuchsia, and a humming bird working on
his red-flower map, yellow pad on my lap,
and a new poem just beginning to tap
on the screened door of invention.
                                    Instead
I've trudged the neon market's swollen aisles
for lettuce, rice, saffron, ripe plums, and fish,
queued politely at the bakeshop for bread.
I'll telephone the liquor store for wine.
Getting and spending and consulting lists,
I am the perfect wife—or I pretend.
            This afternoon I'll drudge, cooking for guests,
slosh through the clammy marsh of peeling shrimp,
the gritty wash of salad greens, contend
with rescuing a burn and smelly trash,
how things will look, the party's fierce detail.
            The rising steam of effort hides the urn
and silences the nightingale. I should
be wandering solitary on the strand,
my locks tossed by a chill wind, but the night
warms with chatter, candlelight, old friends. One,
leaving for home, bestows a kiss and says,
The dinner—the whole evening—was a poem.

Exposure

How can we decide what to keep and what
to give away, what to share and what refuse,
what keep secret, what lay bare? No living thing
slips from the knot of compromise,
not pear tree in prevailing wind
that never finds its perfect ring,
nor vagrant fox that slinks across the field,
nor chipmunk scritching in the wall,
nor phoebes settled on the porch
when we were gone. Brooding now, attached
like buds to stem, too deep to move,
they fret, they flick their tails, they flit from eave
to nest, earnest and plain. We ogle
the small domestic fever of their lives.

Couplets for a Long Marriage

Turn off the lamps and let night in. Explore
me now with tactful darkness to obscure

my freckled, rose-moled skin, the fickle glow
of graying hair, fine wrinkles that betray

the sure inroads of age on every part.
Picture a body glorified by art.

Make me your Odalisque. Touch me and weigh
the imperious comforts of her hip and thigh,

or see me in Olympia's brazen pose,
or in the limber, ripe, unblemished ease

of Renoir's bathers (he, too, had a feel
for breast and buttock). I could be a pastèl

nude Dégas drew a century ago
fresh from her bath, in modest disarray.

Her hair is darkish brown like mine, or close,
And since it hides her face, you might suppose

her me—the skin just touched with a wet brush
and something sharp to tease out surface blush

and dark recess. From now on substitute
for mine, flesh shaped like hers by an astute

sheer layering of hues, a kind of glaze.
See me in that same purposeful haze

that represents and colors truth—
                                    and keep
the canvas fresh till time calls us to sleep.

Invitation to the Dance

In the summer of 1949, Jacques d'Amboise found himself in a clash with a bully who produced a switchblade. "Without even thinking," he recalls. "I did a grand battement—a big kick—knocking his hand and sending the knife flying. The force of my kick spun me around. . . . . I arrived with both feet under me in plié, leaped in the air, and jumped so high my feet kicked down on top of his shoulders, smashing him [flat]."
   —I Was a Dancer

I want to call my sister and chat,
give her the book for her birthday.
"Did you know all that about d'Amboise?"
I'd ask. She was crazy about dance,
and followed its stars.

They more or less took the place
of her teenage movie scrapbooks, endorsed
her passion for Broadway, confirmed her readiness
to splinter any ordinary weekday into shards
of emotional tempest.

But a few years ago
with her customary flair for drama,
she choked on a piece of beef at dinner
and moved on, missing the suspense
of her husband's flailing performance

with Heimlich's maneuver, the sirens,
the elevator, for once on express,
the paramedics, the neighbors
at their gaping doors,
and the way we gathered later

around her hospital bed
like characters in a Puccini opera,
but without their cunning motive;
wanting her only to know
that we had paid attention,

that she was splendid;
wanting her to take a final bow,
wanting her to be aware of our applause.
And then someone noticed
that though the ventilator

and the heart monitor had been turned off,
her feet were still moving
in a slow but rhythmic and purposeful jig,
as if she were warming up for a *grand battement*,
and had decided to dance off stage.

In Memoriam

We breakfast on the splendor of the day,
the meadow's pea-green dazzle, red bird
and goldfinch feeding. Nothing more's required.
      A Luna moth displays her pale moiré

against the glass, but she hangs limp like something lynched,
caught by a web and fastened in the gum
of limbo.
      Redeemers with a kitchen broom,
we knock the threads away from the blue-ceilinged porch.

But how unstick the wings? We lay her sorrowful
and shroudless on the grass. Later she has disappeared.
Her fragile, perfectly silent torment's marred
the morning. Some things are impossible.

Let idle talk and the sweet tedium
of summer's noonday drone provide a requiem.

Getting By

Beautiful Aunt Lily has died.
We decide that you will leave promptly
for the funeral in Chicago
and I will stay home with the children.
Hey, nonny, nonny.

With hardly any gas in the tank
you cruise to LaGuardia, coast down the garage ramp,
push our dry old VW the last few feet into a parking spot
and make the best of United's economy.
Hey, nonny, nonny.

Lily, rescued from Auschwitz forty-four years earlier
but felled finally by cancer,
would have been pleased with the warm family
celebration of her years among us
and the good wishes
for her passage to the next world.
Hey, nonny, nonny.

Sisters, aunts and uncles celebrate, too,
your nick-of-time arrival,
rueful only that you must return to New York
on an early flight the next day.
Hey, nonny, nonny.

That evening, you siphon a couple of quarts of gas
from your brother-in-law's power mower
into a large milk carton, and pack it in your carry-on—
enough to get you and the car to a filling station
not far from the airport and back to Manhattan in time
for an afternoon at the ad agency.
Hey, nonny, nonny

What is it the French say? *Autre temps, autre moeurs.*
What is it you used to say? *It better to be lucky than well-informed.*
With a hey and a ho and a hey nonny no.

Safe Conduct

The second act is over. Tosca's fled
leaving behind a trace of her perfume,
a glass of wine, the knife, and Scarpia dead.
The lights come on; a woman in the row
ahead buttons her coat, pleads her way out:
She has to catch a train; and why pretend?
The last act's simply more than she can bear.
          For her the story ends with love and hope
triumphant, the safe-conduct pass in hand.
She'll trade the 19th-century tapestry
of villainy, deceit, despair, and gloom
for thick suburban wall-to-wall broadloom.
No doubt she similarly trims *Lakmé*,
preserves the lady nursing Gerald's wounds,
spares her the wretched, wasteful suicide;
runs off, too, from Nagasaki before
Pinkerton turns up parading his smug
western bride.
          Tonight, lulled by the wheels,
she dozes her way home to Westchester,
deserted street, snug house, husband asleep.
          But we brave the imperative of art,
exult in Tosca's escape from Scarpia's lust,
seethe at his vile schemes and brute bloodshed,
feel the pull of her defiant leap.
                              She glows
against the tarnished scenery of Rome
teaching us once again what honor claims,
how false is safety's cadence, how close
and rude the dangers that stalk a virtuous heart.

Talk About Love

You never murmur that my eyes are darts
to pierce the stony armor of your breast,
or whisper that beholding me, your heart
does tremble more than if you thought on death,
or voice the perverse hope, indeed the yearning
for my leave-taking and prolonged sojourn
away from home—so sweet is my returning.
And, oh my dear, though I have plainly sworn

to love, I've never counted all the ways
we've left our seasoned kisses in the cup
or tangled arms and legs, noons, midnights, souls,
or probed our faltering way through fortune's maze,
or skidded dumbly from temptation's grip,
trusting each in each; the center holds.

Communiqué

My love—
            I've settled in quite nicely here.
Thanks for the tulips—brilliant red, headstrong,
with siren petals yellow tipped, like tongues
lapping up light or little bits of sun.

I added Albertson's Fresh Flower Food
but even so, tight-closed and lank, they hung
down past the rim like near-sighted old crones
scanning the table top with their lorgnettes.

Next day they were straight up as raw recruits
parading off at someone's awful whim.
(If I had waked up in the night, would I
have heard the pale green stealth of shifting stems?)

A few days later, writhing, disarrayed,
dropping bloody petals, yellow dust,
they crept to horizontal and were gone.
Don't send more—I leave here in a day or so.
Better to let them flourish where they grow.

Choices

Better to part while the body is still
good enough and the heart is sober.
Better to leave while the tapers are dim,
but the party isn't quite over.
Better to own the contraband wins
like a dog that snarfs from the gutter and grins
with perfect indifference to rancor.
Oh, why not slip off of your own free will
without asking anyone's pardon
locking the gate as you go. Above all,
avoid being chased from the garden.

II

*Philosophy is perfectly right in saying
that life must be understood backwards
but then one forgets the other clause—that
it must be lived forward.*
    —Sören Kierkegaard

Joan Didion

Her photo's on the
cover of a magazine.
Turn it over, he insists
wanting to hide
the eyes, those asterisks
that address loss,
taut tendons in her neck,
a witness not to trust.
Mistress of grief
and sacrifice,
she knows the
dying gnawing us.
It's not absurd
for him to be disturbed
She knows what
we don't yet.

Passing On

It is the twenty-fourth of March, the day
when James the First was crowned in 1603,
a day remembered for Houdini's birth
and Jules Verne's death, a day we choose by chance
without fanfare, or magic, or lament
to sign a final will and testament.

Clients, whose relatively modest worth
will be somewhat reduced by legal fees,
we have been invited to see to these
transactions in a lofty conference room
where time is told in paper coffee cups
and we can watch a year of seasons come

and go in just an hour: clouds in convoy,
then a swell of blue, then snow squalls, then sun
breaks richly through. A corner of the park
northwest shows trees preparing for rebirth
as we entrust this ponderous paper ark
to guide the business of life after death.

I, above named Testatrix (gaudy word
that paints a temptress in a topless dance),
being of sound mind, sensibly agree
to transfer to my agent or trustee
authority to act on my behalf
whenever the time comes, to be in charge

of everything—my money, real estate,
my goods and chattels, which include my great
grandmother's gold thimble, the brick wall
in the basement that tends to crumble, the view
from our front porch—a whole array
accounted for. The diabetes gene,

the syncopated heart—they stow away.
We all sign our names on solid lines,

testators and witnesses alike
discussing whether they, when we have gone
to the next world, will have moved on
in this to Madagascar or Maui.

The Styx, where ancient gods swore sacred oaths
is nowhere near, only far away below
the Hudson and beyond, the sea. But here
high on the fortieth floor, we're up against
the firmament, where They must know just when
the next life starts and whether trumpets blow.

History

Tiny paint cans, color-daubed rags,
Xacto knives, airbrush nozzles—
ignoring his cluttered desk, my husband
with a slim sable brush, is painting
the cartridge box of one of Napoleon's dragoons.
A Bothy Band CD croons *Do you love*
an apple? Do you love a pear?
Celtic music an anachronistic surround.
If it weren't for Hitler, I wouldn't be here
watching him. He would be in eastern
Hungary running the family publishing
business. I would be God knows where.

Hustled out of Budapest on a train
heading West—past woods and sidings and
station stops they'd never see again,
my future in-laws caught the last
passenger ship out of Genoa in 1940,
and *the lad with the curly brown hair*
in reckless innocence hugged the rail
hoping to see a U-Boat.

Now I ask him, "Shall we have wine
with dinner?" But like the mythical gods
who slipped easily between their world
and ours, he has wandered away into
the blood and thunder of a19th-century
battle. Having tangled early with history,
he maintains an ongoing relationship
with its dramatic moments and artifacts.

Every shelf harbors an instrument
of war or miniature diorama: Officers
and troopers of the 3rd Eszterhazy Hussar
Regiment preparing for hostilities mill
around a farmyard bidding loved-ones goodbye.
A Messerschmidt rests peacefully next

to a Spitfire. Around the house linger
remnants of long-gone fleets. A Zebec
with extended bowsprit takes up most
of the dresser top; a cross-section of
Nelson's flagship, the H.M.S. Victory,
affixed to the bedroom wall, displays
cannons at the ready, a hold full of barrels.

And lurking just under my husband's
desk, its conning tower and periscope
well hidden, its torpedo compartments still
in pieces, its menacing gray a gleam in his
mind's eye is a U-Boat—soon to be
fitted out for the Battle of the Atlantic.
Our dining room tonight is free of local conflict,
but in the war zone there is shouting and gun fire
drowning out my summons to dinner.

Deceptive Cadence

> *I have to face the sources and the flickering presence of my own*
> *ambivalence as a Jew; the daily, mundane anti-Semitisms of my*
> *entire life.*
> —"Split at the Root" by Adrienne Rich

At the Center for Jewish History
because of terrorists
we wait in a patient line

to pass the security check,
old people, families with children, couples
out for a concert on Saturday night.

We all pass muster and stroll into the theater,
a long narrow room shaped, I think,
like a shoebox.

A Jew box, I say out loud,
headlong words born of rhyme
without gestation as thought.

You nod indulgently
(our family is knit with Jewish yarn),
but your mouth rounds in a small o.

And the jingle turns on me and jeers.
Gas chambers and coffins imitate
its narrow rectangular dimensions.

The tension of its long closed *oo* moans
through the music we have come to hear,
melodies deported with Transylvanian musicians

who never came back, resurrected by gypsies.
Their harmonic minor wanders indiscriminately
through dance and prayer

a Diaspora of augmented seconds
intoning liturgy, celebrating weddings, keening for the dead,
lamentations as comforting as skin.

The concert ends and we rise
to applaud the music makers,
the cimbalom, the zongura, the drums, the strings,

the songs whose deportation failed.
Like football fans whose team has won,
we file out exuberantly

into a wet night,
the rain singing its own small song,
beating its careless time.

Ancestry

At the root of the family tree
they gleam: the offspring of Quakers, pursued
my grandmother says, *for following George Fox
and his circle of Friends.* I picture
Eleanor in a plain pinafore and William,
his little boots scuffed, racing after
the hawk-nosed preacher—Charles II
close behind, his scepter upraised like a bludgeon—

to fling themselves with parents and brothers
on a ship bound straight for the new world,
where, worn by its struggle across the wintry
Atlantic, it sails flimsily up the Delaware
to dock at Chester, Penn's Sylvania.
But, grandmother continues, reciting
by heart from Dorr's History of Bucks County,

the rest of the Baines family died at sea.
Transplanted saplings in a January gale,
William and Eleanor are, according to local
Orphans' Court records, "put out" to
two different "honest" Quaker families.
I try on their loneliness like a costume
and quickly take it off. The girl,
at eleven, is to work "for an annual wage

of 50 shillings," the boy—just seven—
"till he comes of age." Beyond this only
their marriages are documented, together
with a parenthetical note—the name
Baines was early corrupted to Bean.
Questions hover around me like ghosts:
Did they ever meet to grieve, or share a meal,
or talk over their old life in Lancashire?

Had they already sailed by the time James
issued his Declaration of Indulgence?

I cling to them through all my petty trials
in grammar school, the dramatic paranoia
of adolescence, the larger worries
of motherhood. In the most fragile veins
of my body flows their brave, undaunted
blood. They persevered.

It is astonishing that grandmother
found them. A tall, dry old lady,
a principled Methodist, she soon abandons
the family records and turns her energies
to the task of making us churchgoers.
She offers us a dollar to attend
Sunday services. We make fun of her,
the way she sits on the edge of the mattress

at bedtime letting two Milk of Magnesia
tablets dissolve on her tongue because
she believes chewing them suppresses their
effect; the way she wears her sweaters
upside down, the bottom button fastened
at her collar bone, sleeves hanging
loose at her hips like flags that have lost
the wind. We barely know her.

Decades after Abigail Bean Stevens
is called to her fathers, and her typescripts
and notebooks arrive on my doorstep
in large cardboard boxes, I am introduced
to a newly found cousin, who, it turns out,
has taken over the job of family historian.
Skilled in both computer technology
and the intricacies of the Mormons'

genealogical records, he untangles
the snarls of lineage to build
an Ahnentafel Chart, scrupulously
documented with source and citation,
that mirrors grandmother's until it

deviates in the tenth generation.
As far as I have been able to ascertain,
he writes, *there is no connection between*
the Bean family of Georgia and the Baineses
of Weyersdale, Lancashire, England.
How heedlessly he breaks the news
of such a violent divorce. Duped by the
haphazard fraud of a centuries-old
name change, we wanted to believe,
grandmother and I, in two stolid
survivors from whom, for such a long time,
twined our genetic vines. Never mind!
We will adopt them. We will keep them
preserved by time on a high shelf—
family silver to be taken out and polished,
ancient garments with odd stains
handed down and worn to costume parties,
slightly tarnished batons to be brazenly twirled,
faded banners flown from the rooftop.

Seeking Redemption on the Treadmill

"Though none of the enclosed has proven right,"
the letter says, "we wish you all success
in your ongoing work. . ." The pipe-dream dies—
the book tour vanishes; the interview
with Charlie Rose is cancelled. I renounce
the muse and reclaim private life, put on
my Nikes, jog off to the gym in search
of virtue, endorphins, oblivion.
   Three sets of free weights and the thigh machine
propel me to the treadmill, Walkman primed
with Bach—BWV 199—
to drown the blast of the gym's radio.
It seeps through anyway: A woman calls,
asks the DJ to dedicate a song
to Juan Carlos, her lover—no last names
because they've both been married for some time—
not to each other. *My conscience, Lord,*
is wracked with pain, the Walkman interjects
profound despair. The phrase ends letting in
Juan Carlos' song: "I want no othuh lovuh,
I put nothin' above ya. . ." The music
and the sweaty hulk on the next treadmill pound
while the cantata's penitent intones,
Bowed low, beloved God, and full of rue,
I know my guilt. The radio croons through
a rest, "We're happy, it's a fact. Can't
nothin' hold us back. . ."
                                My ritual half-hour
on the machine winds down, and I rejoice
just as Bach's sinner finds his grace
in the Lord's sacrifice. The final chord
yields to the ambient electronic haze.
Outside the locker room, I meet a friend
who earnestly presents me to her coach,
claiming that I'm married to a "perfect man,"
and raised great kids. "The family dog is one
great dog," she adds, while I, at last proved right,

stand by in a serene post-workout glow.
But the loudspeaker argues on, "Don't want
to say I'm sorry, cuz there's nothin' I've
done wrong. . ." Juan Carlos still has miles to go.

Swimming

Starting up from sleep, shrieking,
you wake me at 4:00 a.m.
I was in a submarine
with the dog, you are saying,
and the windows were breaking.
The water was pouring in.
You were safe. You were staying
somewhere else. I pull you back
to the cup of my body
till I feel your breath slowing,
the cold terror running out,
but we are growing older.
I can't keep the waters from rising.

III

...and it is well to superintend the sick, to make them well, to care for the healthy to keep them well, also to care for one's own self, so as to observe what is seemly.
  —Hippocrates, *Precepts*

Sonnet for a Long Marriage

How stale in comfort to remember pain,
recall some trivial laying on of blame,
or small-minded attention to the just
divide of labor—whose turn it was
or who forgot the keys, whose parents must
be cooked for, looked for; and then the effort
to ignore the gnawing bone of anger till
it splinters into grace, forbearance, love.

And now that half a century's gone by,
it simply is enough to be—to covet
and to nurture the familiar trade
of every day, to follow up and down
the tumble of the brain, to walk on these
two feet, with these two hands to knead the bread.

Early Warning System

The dog sniffs up
the morning's secrets
like a reporter on a story,
and we meander behind her
scuffing the pavement.
(Why is he dragging his right foot?)
We pass a new-cut field,
the grass lying about
in small hummocks
offering its warm scent.
Stirred into occasional whirlwinds,
it flies up like salt spray
from a restless sea.
(Why is he dragging his right foot?)
Sounds of distant hammering
and the small commotion of a bee
lecturing alfalfa, Queen Anne's lace.
(Why does his body seem to tilt?)
We pass a neighbor's house
with its display of coneflowers,
a stone wall willy-nillied
into place without cement,
the extra rocks strewn round,
more like a falling monument
than something being built.
The dog's outstripped us.
Reaching home, we find
her fast asleep.
You stumble slightly
On the kitchen step.

Questions for Zeno

It's early days. I think of him as normal.
He pocketed my keys—the kleptomaniac!
Am I in denial or just stoical?

Or maybe long-term love makes me illogical.
Yesterday when he unshelved the bric-a-brac,
I still kept thinking that he might be normal.

It's very clear he isn't always rational:
I found a crystal cocktail glass in his backpack,
but I am trying to be stoical

and act as if it's altogether natural
for him to hang a sandwich from a kitchen rack.
It's early days. I think of him as normal,

but sometimes he seems crazier than usual,
runs off without his cane when he can barely walk.
If I resist denial, forget normal,

might I find life less problematical,
accept this cunning sickness for the cul-de-sac
it is, let go the pretense that he's normal,
give up the vain attempt to be so stoical?

Dinner Out

We munch on steak and fries
in a roadhouse by the river
jollied by the Saturday night buzz from the bar
and Mr. Coffee's gargle.
Here there's been a lunge toward décor:
black and white paper placemats
and wait staff in maroon polo shirts.
Through the porch window we watch the shore
where, ardent with purpose,
a dad and his boy
are casting over and over,
catching nothing but the joy
of a summer evening.
Outside the light fades.
Soon it will be too dark
to see the rapids curling over stones
or, from the muddy beach,
the bulk of an old beaver
lumbering up the opposite bank.
The clink of forks tamed to silence,
we all grasp at that moment of wildness
almost within reach.

Mouse Thoughts

The corner of an idea,
a blur really
that gets away fast,
a way of sharing living
while traveling
in cracks and holes and drawers
where stuff lies raveling.
How shall it be trapped
this vanishing?
With mind enrapt
and fiercely open—
till it's snapped.

Flipping Channels

Eight p.m. eastern finds the marshallin
and her Octavian in langorous dis-
array live at the Met,
                            while sky cam
lays before us, seven central, in all
its deftly groomed detail (the curving track
from first to third as graceful as a farth-
ingale) Progressive Field where Cleveland hosts
the Yankees in midsummer play.
                                    They kiss—
the lovers—banter and delay, a throng
collecting in the hall: the Baron Ochs
with his jeweled box, rival petitioners
to fawn and plead, orphans, hairdresser, cook,
a tenor with a serenade
                            and at
the field, a hot-dog special and the tense
prospect of A-Rod's six-hundredth home run
attract a record crowd, who watch Cleveland
score first. But in the third A-Rod's sac fly
chalks up a transient tie
                            while PBS
presents the princess benching oafish Ochs
to designate Octavian pinch runner
with the silver rose. It seems a kind
of sacrifice, as chancy as a lead-
off walk.
            Now in the sixth the captain hits
to center and Brett Gardner scores. The Yankees
lead 2-1,
            Octavian dazzles Sophie,

knocks the baron out of play while earnest
as a third-base coach, the chaperone
sits by to keep her charge from stealing home.
Two outs dispirit and the fans want more.
New York breaks loose, hits seven in the seventh

and delayed somewhat by one more tenor
serenade, *God bless*, waltz on to join
the blow-out at the inn where Baron Ochs
bedeviled by Octavian's pitching staff
strikes out and blusters off. The princess cedes
the field to youth; Octavian gets the win.
The Indians allowed twelve walks and put
position players on the mound. A-Rod's
six hundredth waits still in the wings. *Yeah, yeah*
recaps the Yankees' manager (ESPN),
Tonight we saw a few strange things.

The Wild Blue Yonder

Every morning after coffee and juice
(not to mention a short row with the voice
of conscience), I staunchly tackle a loose
version of a fitness program designed
to toughen up the Royal Canadian Air
Force years ago. Perhaps it's just the smug

resolve to live a long productive life
that drives the alternate knee-to-chest hugs,
arm-over-the-head curl, legs open wide,
reach for the hip on the opposite side,
then eighty robust shoulder rotations,
and, at last, sixty sit-ups on the rug,

where I rest briefly watching the dogged
propellers of the ceiling fan reproach
my indolence, studying the blue
invitation of sky, the green fanfare
of leaves. It seems important to lie here
trying out the dog's perspective. She takes

her young body for granted, writes her mood
in its calligraphy; feet-in-the-air
bare-belly sleep, the wild gyrations
of the tail, the angled stretch—forepaw to rear.
No need for her to pen a perfect ode.
As for those called, sometimes, *The Great Dead,*

they aren't especially known for zealous heed
to exercise. No one mentions Catullus
folding his toga neatly on a stone
to jog around Lake Garda, Donne in tights
healing his feeble flesh by lifting weights,
or Dickinson shedding her gossamer gown

to practice sit-ups in her sober room.
I'd like to follow their unhealthy lead

(their poems stride robustly on), but they
died young. It's better to be disciplined,
striving forward, fit as a young pilot,
my white silk scarf flying in the wind.

What They Don't Say

lies between them
like dirt on the carpet.
They try to avoid it,
stay in other rooms,
but she needs a book,
he decides to open a window.
Coming and going
they stir it up,
dust in the air,
grime on their shoes.
They track it all over the house.

Auld Acquaintance

From time to time he chooses
to appear in costume.
On Monday, for example, he greeted me
in thinning hair and a newly white beard,
and on Tuesday, he cleverly managed
a tremor in his right hand
as he tried to fit his key in the lock.
On Wednesday, I noticed how overnight
his brows had grown into such thickets
that by Thursday they all but hid
the rheum he must have coaxed
to his eyes in secret.
By Friday, he seemed to have shaved
at least two inches from his height,
but I could see that he was only stooping.
Saturday morning, I found him peering closely
at the *Times* as if he were trying
to decipher a foreign language,
and on Sunday around four in the afternoon,
he capped the subterfuge by falling asleep
in his chair with his mouth open
exhaling in small whistles.

Luckily, I am not fooled by his disguises.

Dolce Far Niente

Through the sash a cool spring afternoon,
the hearth cool, too, though brazen with past blaze,
and Papageno on the radio
bumbling his way into the Temple of Ordeal
while I track Lady Dedlock down London's
desperate streets and wallow in this glut of Art.

But through the window, now, a curious bird
exchanges blossoming pear-tree bough
for feeder, now hides in flickering shade,
now shows himself again, and I forsake
Inspector Bucket's icy chase, to trip
over chairs seeking Audubon's Field Guide.

It's not the usual nuthatch or black-capped
chickadee. Palm warbler? Too hard to see
details; I need binoculars and dart
to the next room, then back again to note a bold
black stripe across the eye, the chestnut crown
that marks the chipping sparrow, settle down

again to read; peripheral vision casts
the sparrow in uneven light. Perhaps
I've not identified. . .where have I set
the glasses down? But blue jays, common scolds,
now bluster him away, allow a grosbeak
to possess the perch, its glamorous rose a mere
façade for gluttony. It guttles Stop
& Shop's best songbird seeds while my own
nerve impulses jumping small synap-
tic clefts collaborate with imprecise
particulates of thought to catch the words
that keep intact this transient paradise.

All That Evening

You woke slowly
from an involuntary nap
on the old Budapest sofa,
and looking at the chair beside mine,
asked softly,
Where did Daddy go?
I had to remind you
that he has been dead for 30 years
but you seemed unconvinced,
and all that evening
he hung about somewhere near.
I wondered
if he meant to fetch you
like a parent
who comes to pick up his child
before the birthday party is over
and consents to a piece of cake
while he waits;
if, for him, death is exile
and he seized this chance
for time off,
hovering in the ether
like a name you can't quite remember.
Unused to easing
roving souls,
we switched off all the lights
and took our aging bodies up to bed.

Incorruptible

The November garden goes to sleep standing up.
Black-eyed Susans, their petals
dingy with time, lean against the stone wall.

Wall-eyed blanket flowers tangle
with faded yarrow at the lawn's edge.

Iris blades, brown-edged with early frost,
wind a shroud over rose canes.
Asters, planted for fall color, pale and stiffen.

Phlox fall in rakish postures, like jackstraws
or withered offerings on a grave.

Grave but raucous heralds of the coming cold,
crows call across the field, combing
dormant grass, finding only stones—

New England stones, harvested like prehistoric tubers
and patched into garden walls.

A leaden beech patched in surgeon's tar,
its roots menacing the stone border,
drops a cover of leaves over moribund green.

Under cover, flowers bury themselves in their roots.
Winter stalks a sacred earthworks.

A gardener appears, clips the daisy stalks
and foxglove, adds them to the mulch.
Snow will make low-slung ghosts of her stunted plants.

Bending low, this latter day Persephone ignores the chill.
Given her charge, in May the dead shall be raised.

For Better or Worse

Today shirt buttons foil their holes,
suspenders twist, glasses go astray.
But yesterday he managed shoes!
each gamely stuck on the wrong foot. Outside,
the year is fading; trees dismiss their leaves.

An unknown messenger has rung our bell,
returned a battered briefcase with a note:
Found on the street. Inside, I find the checks
that disappeared last week. An autumn
wind spins trash along the walk.

Ten days ago, he managed to escape the aide,
walked twenty blocks without his cane,
fell down—into the grace of strangers.
I picked him up at Bellevue, brought him home
where early dusk stalks me from room to room.

Last summer when I read that book called "Wild:
From Lost to Found. . ." by Cheryl Strayed,
I wished for some trial like an Outward Bound
to test my strength. I didn't know
I'd find it here so close at hand.
.

And I have learned to wander with the trail
read weather signs, patch things that shred with wear,
keep going even when the visibility is poor,
exploit some lucky positives.
(I know there are no medals for old wives.)

IV

*...we leave behind a bit of ourselves
wherever we have been.*
      —Edmond Haraucourt, *Rondel de l' Adieu*

Babblewacky

Autopsy Report X-4113, Albert Einstein
College of Medicine, April 26, 1989.

Invisible the senile plaques
that mire and hamper synthesis;
all gluey is the neural flax
entangled in paralysis.

Along the ságittal divide
opaque leptómenínges twine;
the sulci loom especially wide,
the cortical gray mantle's thin.

"Beware gloméruli, my friends,
and amyloid angiopathy!
Beware gliosis and defend
against the gyri's atrophy!"

Powerless here the vorpal blade
to fight the mind's furtive decay.
We cannot amputate the head. . .
nor can the microscope survey

Hirano bodies, ghost neurons,
the neurofibrillary snarl,
the fiendish gimble of the brain—
while body harbors still the soul.

Invisible the senile plaques
growing stealthily like moss,
petrifying layers of chalk,
each tangled gain, another loss.

The Small Hours

Are huge, an eight-lane highway
with no traffic.
A lone hitchhiker.
Now beyond the entrance ramp
there's a steady light
and expectations leap.
But it's only the reflection
in a deserted plate-glass office park
of a cobra-headed
sodium-vapor roadway lamp.
Morning stubbornly
withholds her help.

Bedlam

He lies still for his bed bath
groggy with sleep,
soothed by warm water,
careless of the most personal touch,
the generous daubs of ointment.
We bestow five or six pills
every three hours, urged in
with chocolate pudding.
We brush his teeth after meals;
we wash him again at bedtime,
comfort him with three pillows
and a view of the moon.
His body is ours, but his mind
escapes us at every opportunity.
At breakfast, he pours milk
in the toaster and butters his plate.
He gets his suitcase out of the
closet and packs two T-shirts
and a ceramic sculpture of
a voluptuous nude.
At lunch he tells me
he qualifies for the bike race.
He is convinced that someone
has stolen our pictures off the walls
and given us back copies.
Our living room is full of ghosts
with whom he has daily
conversations. One of them
is someone with my name.
when I ask who she is, he says,
"My ex-wife. Little pieces of us
keep breaking off."

I hear you, old man.
Remind me who you were.

The bony corset
of anger binds me tightly.
Sleep cannot get in.

Long-Term Care

> "Let's be a comfortable couple and take care of each other! And if we
> should get deaf, or lame, or blind, or bedridden, how glad we shall be that
> we have somebody we are fond of always to talk and sit with!"
> —Tim Linkenwater's proposal to Miss LaCreevy
> from *Nicholas Nickleby* by Charles Dickens.

How full their lives in these last years,
with the raw material of complaint
as if nature, hating emptiness,
contrives the daily scratch of discontent.
They toss about in fifty years of litter.
Everything's a mess. She hits him with her cane.
He writes to us in tiny, shaky letters.
A neighbor whispers that he's often mean,
their love eclipsed by neediness
that neither can allay, his body frail,
her mind: marriage in a fun-house glass.
This, it turns out, is when you go to Hell—
before you die. Lucifer's enclave,
a place it's nothing much to leave.

The Night of the Generals

The night is dark with heavy rain.
He doesn't want to go to bed;
he's moving toward the door again;
he needs the car, won't be denied.

He doesn't want to go to bed.
He has to drive to Texas NOW.
He needs the car, won't be denied.
I've got to keep him in somehow.

He has to drive to Texas NOW
to meet the German generals.
I've got to keep him in somehow.
He wants to be professional,

to meet the German generals.
He served as Duty Officer;
he wants to be professional,
the 3rd Battalion's well-wisher.

He served as Duty Officer,
a tribute to the uniform,
the 3rd Battalion's well-wisher.
I'm anxious to preserve some norm.

A tribute to the uniform,
to him the meeting's critical.
I'm anxious to preserve some norm.
My argument's too rational.

To him the meeting's critical.
He's not allowed to drive so far;
my argument's too rational
and we no longer have a car.

He's not allowed to drive so far,
(do neighbors overhear our row?)

and we no longer have a car.
The army's long behind him now.

Do neighbors overhear our row?
What luck! Our daughter's on the phone.
(The army's long behind him now.)
She says the Brass want to postpone.

What luck—our daughter's on the phone.
She says the driving is unsafe,
the generals say that they'll postpone,
and so the meeting is called off.

She says that driving is unsafe.
He settles down; she makes it plain
they want to call the meeting off.
The night is dark with heavy rain.

Undertow

What I hate most
about the beach
besides the brutality
of the sun
is being caught
by the waves
and boiled in the sand.
And now I am in it
every day:
caught and boiled
over and over,
and over and over.

Anger

Scorches the heart.
It swelters and smolders,
is useful, perhaps, to soldiers;
the sin with the sharpest edges,
the only one
in which God indulges.
And what of Job
whose riches made him smug?
His wrath, a kind of pilgrimage,
restored God's patronage.
Anger in beasts
is fearsome to the watcher.
But birds of prey
attack in hunger
not in rancor.
How then assess the slug,
the caterpillar, snail?
Exempt from bestial violence,
they leave their silent trails
in Braille, are never called on
to explain
if rage is reflex,
choice, or cry of pain.

Wasp Leg(s)*

Cardinal, not ordinal,
they may give rise to waste and carnage.
A soft answer can preempt some damage;
the story of *The Emperor's New Clothes,*
we heed to our advantage.
The meek will surely shun
all possible corrupting villanage
but ordinary mortals often yield
to subterfuge, or privilege,
or foolish courage and indulge;
and who is sage
enough to judge such slippage?
Seven part-time jobs
that lack the interdiction of Commandments,
are they deadly sacrilege
or simply feelings that are hard to manage?

Mnemonic for the seven deadly sins: Wrath, avarice, sloth, pride, lust, envy, greed.

Aubade

Hollows in the mattress
like the outline of a body in the sand,
my breasts make circles,
and my legs, an empty A.
I turn into a **c**edilla
and you, familiar with letters,
hug its knees.
Live matter, not quite awake,
we dally in a crooked H
to slow the steady press of day.

Domestic Violence

Widow: a hollow, sallow word,
a window without view or sun,
someone old, confined and prim.
And yet I yearn to become one,
to quench the rage that lunges daily
from my tight-locked box of failings
because the milk has spilled,
the newspaper is torn to shreds,
he's waked me from sound sleep.
Raising my arm with vengeful will,
I break my wrist on the bed rail.
I'm mean, inept, and without grace.
Shrewishness: a stage of grief;
pieces of us keep breaking off.
Wondrously rational, he says
I'm not always myself, remember.
More and more we live with strangers.
He was my ritual, my drink, my bread.
Still loving him, I wish him dead.

Connoisseurs

He falls on the front steps
leaving brilliant red drops
on the cement. He falls
in the dining room
flapping and wriggling on the hook
of Parkinson's,
unable to right himself.
He falls out of bed
and lies on his back
like a stunned beetle.
Though he is no longer
my robust, barrel-chested guy,
I can't lift him.
I never used to fall, he says.
Now I'm a connoisseur.
Days later,
going up a long flight of stairs
he slips weakly to his side,
pinned at an angle
by the rising treads.
The EMTs come yet again
and take him to the hospital
where a UTI is diagnosed.

His roommate
on the bladder-issues floor
is a gaunt Latino who parades
vigorously through the halls
proclaiming, in spite of the bloody
catheter bag he drags with him,
that he is 92 years old and
much too healthy to be where he is.
He is accompanied
on these journeys
by a retinue of admiring
relatives and friends
who envelop him in

incessant spirited chatter.

At rest from time to time
in the next bed, basking
in the occasional photo-op, he wears
black, wrap-around Ray-Bans,
and preens his wild, white hair,
a connoisseur of marooned glamor.

I leave them,
these stalwarts of public care,
and go back home—
to my childhood voice asking,
Will everything be ok?
to my empty bed,
to my rickety holding on.

Not Choking but Coughing

(After Stevie Smith)

We took him in trembling and coughing.
We wanted cough syrup, a pill.
The ER was like a bus station,
Busy and dingy and chill.

People kept coming and going
An impromptu sickness bazaar,
We felt isolated, neglected.
There were curious stains on the floor.

They insisted he must be admitted.
I argued, seething and chafing.
He was sicker than we'd suspected,
They said, and choking, not coughing.

They gave him a hospital bed
And hooked him to two wily tubes,
Ignored the routine of his Parkinson's meds,
And forbade the intake of food.

Poor guy, he always loved eating
And abhorred the sight of purée,
So after six days of their expert neglect,
I took him—not choking but coughing—away.

Peelings

They are never the same.
Bananas, stringy, black
on sidewalk grit or upright
and asymmetrical like small
octopuses; eggshells, benign
but splintered sharps,
their delicate membranes
a kind of chicken caul;
and alligator pears, elliptical
with pebbled rinds like little boats.
My grandfather could skin
an orange with a knife
in one continuous
graceful twirl.
When you peel me away at last
how will I fall?

Hereafter

Certain theologians assure us that the body's resurrection begins at the moment of death. They know too much. God has His reasons for keeping death under wraps.
—The Notebooks of Anna Kamienska

Lay me out on cinderblocks,
at my head two carrot sticks,
stems for legs, my feet are roses,
bind my jaw with dental flosses.
Let swans tow me on my way,
their necks like vacuum-cleaner hoses.
Clutching a phantasmal token,
I'll queue on a suspension bridge
where only Esperanto's spoken
and incorporeals try to fathom
the divine process of Heaven,
how they take away your face,
dole out fresh skin, fingerprints,
strip the soul of memory,
leaving instinct still in place,
send it back into the race.
Invisible I'll circulate
till molecules evaporate.

Letting Go

His dying (though we were unsure) was slow.
He didn't seem to yield at once to something dire,
rather to let the pieces of his life just go.
He couldn't drive or take in what he read.
His cheerful baritone became a gentle rasp;
he couldn't walk or feed himself or know
reality from dream. But like some trades,
the losses brought chance gains: he chatted face
to face with people that I couldn't see,
once spied a flock of rabbis dancing down
an empty street. When at the last he lay
quite still, unvexed by so much lost control,
his breathing stuttered by short gasps,
we knew the body guarded still the soul.

Or maybe it's the other way around.
Perhaps it is the soul's charge and intent
through life to keep the body sound
but which, at last, fails to defeat large mortal accident,
undo ecclesiastical command.
We sat there till the body, spent, withdrew.
The soul, I think, stayed by.
I stroked his brow but wish I'd held his hand.
They wrapped him simply in a plain white sheet
as artists have drawn Christ descended from the cross
(some things don't change, the wrapping tightly furled)
and took him off, two drivers, an old van.
My cavalier, my balm—he claims me still—
left us cast off with all the too much world.

Now,

where have you taken
your blessed soul, and how shall I find it?
I hope you are exploring your new dwelling place
with the same sense of wonder
you brought to living.
It is wrong for you to be deprived
of this magnificent, messy world—
green fields,
marauding mice in the kitchen,
the tapestry of red and yellow leaves underfoot,
the labor of raking them,
deer in the woods,
the malign visit of a tick,
the company of dogs,
the bear at the compost bin.
Shall I look for you
in the secret place of the most High
under the light of the Almighty?
Or in the books on your shelves,
in dreams, in old letters,
in my thirst for your touch?
Rather, I must sing now
the mysterious melody of time,
stubbornly, until eternity
is no longer out of reach.

ACKNOWLEDGEMENTS

Grateful acknowledgement is made to the editors of the following journals, chapbook, and anthology where these poems first appeared.

Atlanta Review: "Flipping Channels"
The Best of Toadlily Press: "Talk About Love"
The Dark Horse: "Seeking Redemption on the Treadmill"
Heliotrope: "The Life of a Poet," "Safe Conduct"
The MacGuffin: "Long Term Care"
Plume: "Invitation to the Dance," "Domestic Violence," "All That Evening"
Sightline, Toadlily Press: "Babblewacky," "Exposure," "In Memoriam," "Of Body and Mind," "Swimming"
Songs of Eretz: "Deceptive Cadence," "Passing On"
Southwest Review: "Communique" (Second prize winner in Morton Marr Poetry Prize Contest)

The author would like to thank the Ragdale Foundation for the support which allowed her to write many of these poems.

Thanks to Molly Peacock for her friendship, her guidance, and her example.

Very special thanks also to Meredith Trede and Brad Kenyon for their encouragement, reading, editing, and technical support, without which this book couldn't have been completed.

Carol Stevens Kner's poems have appeared in *Western Humanities Review,* the *Paris Review, Heliotrope, North American Review, Southwest Review, The Dark Horse,* and other journals. Her chapbook, *Exposure,* was published by Toadlily Press. She served for many years as managing editor and staff writer at *PRINT Magazine* and has written articles for the *Encyclopedia of World Art, Connaissance des Arts,* and the *New Book of Knowledge.* Several of her poems have been set to music by American composer Christopher Berg and performed in concert in New York City and Paris. She has held residency fellowships at Ragdale. Carol graduated from Smith College. She has studied with Richard Howard, Marie Ponsot, Molly Peacock, and Richard Wilbur.

www.ingramcontent.com/pod-product-compliance
Lightning Source LLC
Chambersburg PA
CBHW021157090426
42740CB00008B/1132